THINKING TIME

365 inspiring, amusing and thought-provoking
quotes to get you through the year

JEM VANSTON

HOW TO USE THIS BOOK

This book is ideal for those wishing to take some time out of a busy day for a moment's **'Intelligent Mindfulness'**, reflection and thinking time.

Some people read the whole book through from front to back, perhaps even in one sitting. Others just like to dip in at random now and again. But many readers choose to read a quote a day and thus develop a daily habit of mindfulness in their lives. This can be both calming and empowering, uplifting and positive, and help to promote well-being.

Select a quote a day, in order, for every date of the year, or simply choose a page at random. Focus on that quote as your inspiration for that day.

You may find it helpful to mouth the words or speak them softly, once or several times. Deep breathing exercises can promote calmness and relaxation while doing this. Keep the book with you during the day, or write the quote down. Read and reflect on it in spare moments, perhaps jotting down any ideas and feelings you may have. Let your thoughts wander and take you along. Enjoy the ride!

How long you focus on one quote is up to you – it can be a few seconds or even minutes. Ultimately, you have to find what is right for you. For me, a minimum of thirty seconds per quote offers an opportunity for real focus, to centre oneself and clear one's head. I know I always feel better after this 'Intelligent Mindfulness'. When I first tried it, I remember being surprised at how such a simple technique could have such a positive impact, promoting clarity, calmness and well-being.

As well as being a useful tool for daily meditation, this book is a resource for teaching and public speaking. A well-chosen quote can provide a good starting point, and clear focus, to any speech in any context.

All quotations, of course, have an original context and author, as detailed at the foot of every page – but the context of every quote in this book is also the life of the reader. Ultimately, what each quote means will vary according to your lived experience and way of seeing.

Of course, how you read and use this book is up to you, the reader – which is exactly as it should be. Enjoy your Thinking Time!

AUTHOR NOTE

I started to compile the quotes in this book during what was a challenging period of bereavement and illness. At that time, reading – or writing – fiction (or non-fiction) held little appeal.

So, instead, I began reading through quotations – many thousands of them – which, as I soon discovered, can be enjoyably addictive!

The way thoughts, ideas and emotions can be expressed so succinctly in quotations is something I found both inspiring and thought-provoking.

I then used them to develop what I call **'Intelligent Mindfulness'**, by which I mean a way of being mindful by focusing on a single quote which holds within it a certain wisdom or truth, and which takes on meaning in the context of the reader's life. I certainly felt better for this endeavour, learning to take time out to clear my head and focus every day, by using the method outlined previously. It's so simple to do, and can be calming, motivating, insightful, inspiring and instructive, as well as educational.

The sort of mindfulness books which include overtly spiritual/religious quotes never held any appeal for me, and neither did the more slushy and schmaltzy self-help quote collections. So, being a self-starter with a rather independent streak, I decided to compile my own.

Needless to say, this is a very personal collection of my favourite quotes, so they necessarily reflect both my education and life experience, my tastes and interests, as well as my sense of humour.

There is much debate on attribution of quotes, and I have gone with my instincts regarding this, often following a general consensus, but sometimes pointing out a misattribution. Translations of quotes not originally in English can vary, too, and I have again used my judgement in selecting the version I feel best conveys the meaning of each.

I hope you enjoy your **'Thinking Time'** and **'Intelligent Mindfulness'**.

Author page: www.vanston.co.uk

Twitter: @ThinkingQuotes7

January 1

It's never too late to be who you might have been.

George Eliot, (Mary Ann Evans), British author, 1819-1880

January 2

Begin at the beginning and go on till you come to the end: then stop.

Lewis Carroll, (Charles Dodgson), British author of Alice in Wonderland, 1832-1898

January 3

Whatever you can do, or dream you can, begin it. Boldness has genius, power and magic in it.

Johann Wolfgang von Goethe, German writer and statesman, 1749-1832

January 4

If you're going through hell, keep going.

*Sir Winston Churchill, British Prime Minister
and writer, 1874-1965*

January 5

Believe nothing to be impossible.

Amy Johnson, British aviatrix pioneer,
1903-1941

January 6

Learn from yesterday, live for today, hope for tomorrow.

Albert Einstein, German-born theoretical physicist, 1879-1955

January 7

When you get a sinking feeling, don't worry. It's probably because you're hungry.

A.A. Milne, British author of
Winnie-the-Pooh, 1882-1956

January 8

Ageing is an extraordinary process where you become the person you should have been.

David Bowie, (David Jones), British singer-songwriter and actor, 1947-2016

January 9

If you can dream it, you can do it.

Walt Disney, American animator and film producer, 1901-1966

January 10

A journey of a thousand miles must begin with a single step.

Attributed to Lao Tzu, semi-legendary Chinese Taoist philosopher, exact dates unknown but 6th-4th century BC.

January 11

Do just once what others say you can't do, and you will never pay attention to their limitations again.

James Cook, British explorer, cartographer and Royal Navy Captain, 1728-1779

January 12

Smile every morning.
Get it over with.

Sir Ken Dodd, British comedian,
1927-2018

January 13

The one thing you have that nobody else has is you. Your voice, your mind, your story, your vision. So write and draw and build and play and dance and live only as you can.

Neil Gaiman, British author, 1960-

January 14

Sometimes even to live is an act of courage.

Seneca (Lucius Annaeus), Roman Stoic philosopher and statesman, 4BC-65AD

January 15

Very little is needed to make a happy life; it is all within yourself, in your way of thinking.

Marcus Aurelius, Roman emperor and Stoic philosopher, 121-180AD

January 16

Twenty years from now you will be more disappointed by the things that you didn't do than by the ones you did do.

Mark Twain, (Samuel Clemens), American author and humorist, 1835-1910

January 17

Courage is being scared to death but saddling up anyway.

John Wayne, (Marion Morrison), American film actor, 1907-1979

January 18

It always seems impossible until it's done.

Nelson Mandela, anti-apartheid activist and
South African President, 1918-2013

January 19

It takes courage to grow up and become
who you really are.

E.E. Cummings, US poet, 1894-1962

January 20

Today is the tomorrow you were so worried about yesterday.

Sir Anthony Hopkins,
British (Welsh) actor, 1937-

January 21

Science will save us,
but art will heal us.

Anonymous

January 22

It is better to have dreamed a thousand dreams that never were than never to have dreamed at all.

Alexander Pushkin, Russian poet, playwright and novelist, 1799-1837

January 23

Dreams are the seeds of action.

Donald Crowhurst, inventor, businessman and sailor, 1932-1969

January 24

Hope is the fuel of progress and fear is the prison in which you put yourself.

Tony Benn (Anthony Neil Wedgwood), British politician and writer, 1925-2014

January 25

The biggest mistake people make in life is not trying to make a living at doing what they enjoy most.

Malcolm Forbes, American publisher and businessman, 1919-1990

January 26

When you're finished changing,
you're finished.

*Benjamin Franklin, American Founding
Father, polymath, author, politician, inventor
and scientist, 1705-1790*

January 27

Jogging is for people who aren't intelligent enough to watch television.

Victoria Wood, British comedian, composer and screenwriter, 1953-2016

January 28

The world is like a grand staircase, some are going up and some are going down.

Samuel Johnson, British writer and lexicographer, 1709-1784

January 29

One life is all we have and we live it as we believe in living it. But to sacrifice what you are and to live without belief, that is a fate more terrible than dying.

Joan of Arc, French heroine and Catholic saint, c. 1412-1431

January 30

The greatness of a nation and its moral progress can be judged by the way its animals are treated.

Mahatma Gandhi (Mohandas Karamchand), Indian nationalist, lawyer and ethicist, 1869-1948

January 31

I have a new philosophy. I am only going to dread one day at a time.

Charles M. Schulz, US cartoonist and creator of Charlie Brown, 1922-2000

February 1

Most women set out to change a man, and when they have changed him they do not like him.

Marlene Dietrich, German actress and singer, 1901-1992

February 2

What I am looking for is a blessing not in disguise.

Jerome K. Jerome, British author and humorist, 1859-1927

February 3

Deep down, the young are lonelier than the old.

Anne Frank, German-Dutch diarist, 1929-1945

February 4

Common sense and a sense of humour are the same thing, moving at different speeds. A sense of humour is just common sense, dancing.

Clive James, Australian author and broadcaster, 1939-2019

February 5

If everybody is thinking alike, then somebody isn't thinking.

George S. Patton, US World War II General, 1885-1945

February 6

Nothing in life is to be feared; it is only to be understood.

Marie Skoldowska Curie, Polish-French scientist, 1867-1934

February 7

No one is useless in this world who lightens the burdens of another.

Charles Dickens, British author, 1812-1870

February 8

Your assumptions are your windows on the world. Scrub them off every once in a while, or the light won't come in.

Isaac Asimov, Russian-born American science fiction author, 1920-1992

February 9

Dying is easy, it's living that scares me to death.

Annie Lennox, British (Scottish) musician and singer-songwriter, 1954 -

February 10

That men do not learn very much from the lessons of history is the most important of all the lessons that history has to teach.

Aldous Huxley, British writer and philosopher, 1894-1963

February 11

Most of the important things in the world have been accomplished by people who have kept on trying when there seemed to be no hope at all.

Dale Carnegie, American self-help guru and writer, 1888-1955

February 12

It is not the strongest of the species that survive, nor the most intelligent, but the one most responsive to change.

Charles Darwin, British naturalist, biologist, geologist and author, 1809-1882

February 13

It's best to know what you're looking for before you look for it.

A.A. Milne, British author of
Winnie-the-Pooh, 1882-1956

February 14

Never love anyone who treats you like
you're ordinary.

*Oscar Wilde, Anglo-Irish poet and playwright,
1854-1900*

February 15

Love is not looking in each other's eyes, but looking together in the same direction.

Antoine de Saint-Exupéry, French writer and aviator, 1900-1944

February 16

There is only one happiness in this life, to love and be loved.

George Sand, (Amantine Dupin), French author, 1804-1876

February 17

There is no love sincerer than the love of food.

George Bernard Shaw, Irish playwright, 1856-1950

February 18

Love is the realisation that something other than oneself is real.

Iris Murdoch, Irish-British author and philosopher, 1920-1999

February 19

Courage is resistance to fear, mastery of fear, not absence of fear.

Mark Twain, (Samuel Clemens), American author and humorist, 1835-1910

February 20

Sex: the thing that takes up the least amount of time and causes the most amount of trouble.

John Barrymore, American actor, 1882-1942

February 21

I don't need a friend who changes when I change and who nods when I nod; my shadow does that much better.

Plutarch, (Lucius Mestrius Plutarchus), Greek-Roman philosopher and biographer, 46-119AD

February 22

If you don't say what you think then you
kill your unborn self.

*Jordan B. Peterson, Canadian
psychologist and author, 1962-*

February 23

If any of you cry at my funeral, I'll never speak to you again.

Stan Laurel, (Arthur Stanley Jefferson), British comedy actor, writer and director, 1890-1965

February 24

Love does not begin and end the way we seem to think it does. Love is a battle, love is war; love is growing up.

James Baldwin, American author and activist, 1924-1987

February 25

Only the educated are free.

Epictetus, Greek Stoic philosopher,
50-138AD

February 26

Colours are the smiles of nature.

*Leigh Hunt, British poet
and essayist, 1784-1859*

February 27

When I grow up, I still want to be a director.

Steven Spielberg, American film director, producer and writer, 1946-

February 28

The best prophet of the future is the past.

George Gordon, Lord Byron, British
Romantic poet, 1788-1824

February 29
LEAP YEAR

Once every four years, so 2024, 2028 etc.

Don't cry because it's over, smile because it happened.

Anonymous. Often misattributed to US children's author Dr Seuss. Used by the author of this book in 'A Cat Called Dog 2 – the One with the Kittens' (2017)

March 1

Do the little things in life.

*St. David (Dewi Sant), Bishop of Mynyw (St.
David's) and patron saint of Wales,
c. 6th century AD*

March 2

If you obey all the rules, you miss all the fun.

Katharine Hepburn, American actress, 1907-2003

March 3

The way to know life is to love many things.

Vincent Van Gogh, Dutch painter, 1853-1890

March 4

If you cannot get rid of the family skeleton,
you may as well make it dance.

*George Bernard Shaw, Irish playwright,
1856-1950*

March 5

Pleasure of love lasts but a moment. Pain of love lasts a lifetime.

Bette Davis, American actress, 1908-1989

March 6

Long experience has told me that to be criticised is not always to be wrong.

Anthony Eden, British Prime Minister, 1897-1977

March 7

We deem those happy who, from the experience of life, have learned to bear its ills, without being overcome by them.

Juvenal, (Decimus Junius Juvenalis), Roman poet, exact dates unknown, 1st-2nd centuries AD

March 8

Happiness depends on ourselves.

Aristotle, Greek philosopher,
384-322BC

March 9

We're born alone, we live alone, we die alone.
Only through our love and friendship can we
create the illusion for the moment that we are not
alone.

*Orson Welles, US film director, producer,
screenwriter and actor, 1915-85*

March 10

Success is getting what you want.
Happiness is wanting what you get.

*Dale Carnegie, American self-help guru and
writer, 1888-1955*

March 11

The loneliest moment in someone's life is when they are watching their whole world fall apart, and all they can do is stare blankly.

F. Scott Fitzgerald, American author, 1896-1940

March 12

The trees that are slow to grow bear the best fruit.

Molière, (Jean-Baptiste Poquelin), French playwright, 1622-1673

March 13

If it is not scary, it is not worth doing

*Rhys Ifans, British (Welsh) actor,
1967-*

March 14

You don't learn to walk by following rules.
You learn by doing, and by falling over.

*Sir Richard Branson, British businessman and
entrepreneur, 1950 -*

March 15

It is our choices that show what we truly are, far more than our abilities.

J.K. Rowling, British author of the Harry Potter books, 1965-

March 16

We can't solve problems by using the same kind of thinking we used when we created them.

Albert Einstein, German-born theoretical physicist, 1879-1955

March 17

It is not because things are difficult that we do not dare; it is because we do not dare that they are difficult.

Seneca (Lucius Annaeus), Roman Stoic philosopher and statesman, 4BC-65AD

March 18

There is no greater harm than that of time wasted.

Michelangelo (di Lodovico Buonarroti Simoni), Italian sculptor, painter and architect, 1475-1564

March 19

The ladder of success must be set upon something solid before you can start to climb.

Voltaire, (François-Marie Arouet), French writer and philosopher, 1694-1778

March 20

When things are bad, we take comfort in the thought that they could always be worse. And when they are, we find hope in the thought that things are so bad that they have to get better.

Malcolm Forbes, American publisher and businessman, 1919-1990

March 21

Start where you are. Use what you have.
Do what you can.

Arthur Ashe, US tennis player (1975
Wimbledon champion), 1943-1993

March 22

Our greatest glory is not in never failing, but in rising every time we fail.

Confucius, (Kong Fuzi), Chinese philosopher, 551-479BC

March 23

The way to get started is to quit talking and begin doing.

Walt Disney, American animator and film producer, 1901-1966

March 24

Life is pleasant. Death is peaceful. It's the transition that is troublesome.

Isaac Asimov, Russian-born American science fiction author, 1920-1992

March 25

Love lasteth as long as the money
endureth.

*William Caxton, British writer, pioneer of the
printing press and book seller,
1422-1491*

March 26

Music is a higher revelation than all
wisdom and philosophy.

*Ludwig van Beethoven, German composer,
1770-1827*

March 27

If I have made any valuable discoveries, it has been owing more to patient attention than to any other talent.

Sir Isaac Newton, British physicist, mathematician and author, 1643-1727

March 28

Computers are useless. They can only give you answers.

Pablo Picasso, Spanish painter,
sculptor and ceramicist, 1881-1973

March 29

What you leave behind is not what is engraved in stone monuments, but what is woven into the lives of others.

Pericles, Greek statesman and orator, 495-429BC

March 30

Censorship is to art as lynching is to justice.

Henry Louis Gates Jr., US professor of African-American Studies, 1950-

March 31

Be sure, then, that we have nothing to fear in death. Someone who no longer exists cannot suffer, or differ in any way from someone who has not been born.

Lucretius, (Titus Lucretius Carus), Roman poet and philosopher, c. 99-55BC

April 1

Always laugh when you can. It's a cheap medicine.

George Gordon, Lord Byron, British Romantic poet, 1788-1824

April 2

Laughter is the sun that drives winter from the human face.

Victor Hugo, French author,
1802-1885

April 3

Whatever you have, spend less.

Samuel Johnson, British writer and lexicographer, 1709-1784

April 4

Death is the most convenient time to tax rich people.

David Lloyd George, British (Welsh) Prime Minister, 1863-1945

April 5

All I ask is the chance to prove that money can't make me happy.

Spike Milligan (Terence Alan), British comedian and writer, 1918-2002

April 6

A wise man should have money in his head, but not in his heart.

Jonathan Swift, Anglo-Irish satirist and author, 1667-1745

April 7

If you owe a bank a hundred pounds, you have a problem. But if you owe a million, it has.

John Maynard Keynes, British Economist, 1883-1946

April 8

Try again. Fail again. Fail better.

Samuel Beckett, Irish-French playwright,
1906-1989

April 9

Don't be self-absorbed. Be absorbed in the world around you. It's more interesting.

Prince Philip, Duke of Edinburgh, consort to Queen Elizabeth II, 1921-2021

April 10

A bank is a place that will lend you money
if you can prove you don't need it.

*Bob Hope (Leslie Townes), British-born
American comedian and actor,1903-2003*

April 11

Man is an animal that makes bargains; no other animal does this – no dog exchanges bones with another.

Adam Smith, British (Scottish) economist and philosopher, 1723-1790

April 12

A good decision is based on knowledge and not on numbers.

Plato, Greek philosopher, c. 427-347BC

April 13

If you are afraid of being lonely, don't try to be right.

Jules Renard, French author, 1864-1910

April 14

Being entirely honest with yourself is a good exercise.

Sigmund Freud, Austrian founder of psychoanalysis, 1856-1939

April 15

A quiet conscience makes one strong.

Anne Frank, German-Dutch diarist,
1929-1945

April 16

Enjoy your creativity.

*Sir Ken Dodd, British comedian, (in a 2014
letter to the author), 1927-2018*

April 17

All our knowledge has its origins in our perceptions.

Leonardo da Vinci, Italian artist, inventor and polymath, 1452-1519

April 18

If you're going to tell people the truth, be funny or they'll kill you.

Billy Wilder, Polish-American film director and screenwriter, 1906-2002

April 19

Ability is nothing without opportunity.

Napoleon Bonaparte, French military leader and emperor, 1769-1821

April 20

It does not matter how slowly you go, so long as you do not stop.

Confucius, (Kong Fuzi), Chinese philosopher, 551-479BC

April 21

It's all to do with the training: you can do a lot if you're properly trained.

Queen Elizabeth II, British monarch and head of state, 1926-

April 22

The world is a comedy to those that think,
a tragedy to those that feel.

Horace Walpole, British politician and author,
1717-1797

April 23

He who stops being better stops being good.

Oliver Cromwell, British military and political leader, Lord Protector of Britain, 1599-1658

April 24

You will never find happiness if you continue to search for what happiness consists of. You will never live if you are looking for the meaning of life.

Albert Camus, French author and philosopher, 1913-1960

April 25

A day without laughter is a day wasted.

Charlie Chaplin, British comic actor, film director, screenwriter, composer, 1889-1977

April 26

In no great while you will be no-one and nowhere, and nothing that you now behold will be in existence, nor will anyone now alive. For it is in the nature of all things to change and alter and perish, so that others may arise in their turn.

Marcus Aurelius, Roman emperor and Stoic philosopher, 121-180AD

April 27

Nothing will work unless you do.

Maya Angelou, American poet, author and activist, 1928-2014

April 28

The greatest wealth is health.

Virgil (Publius Vergilius Maro), Roman poet, 70-19BC

April 29

By working faithfully eight hours a day, you may eventually get to be boss and work twelve hours a day.

Robert Frost, American poet, 1874-1963

April 30

If I'd observed all the rules, I'd never have got anywhere.

Marilyn Monroe, (Norma Jeane Mortenson), American actress and singer, 1926-1962

May 1

If you're going to kick authority in the teeth, you might as well use both feet.

Keith Richards, British musician, guitarist and songwriter, 1943-

May 2

It takes a great deal of bravery to stand up to our enemies, but just as much to stand up to our friends.

J.K. Rowling, British author of the Harry Potter books, 1965-

May 3

You may have to fight a battle more than once to win it.

Margaret Thatcher, British Prime Minister, 1925-2013

May 4

I prefer liberty with danger than peace with slavery.

Jean-Jacques Rousseau, French writer and political philosopher, 1712-1778

May 5

The best way to make your dreams come true is to wake up.

Paul Valéry, French poet and philosopher, 1871-1945

May 6

You must be the change you wish to see in the world.

Mahatma Gandhi (Mohandas Karamchand), Indian nationalist, lawyer and ethicist, 1869-1948

May 7

I'd rather be hated for who I am, than loved for who I am not.

Kurt Cobain, American musician, singer and songwriter, 1967-1994

May 8

Accept the challenges so that you can feel the exhilaration of victory.

George S. Patton, US World War II General, 1885-1945

May 9

As soon as you trust yourself, you will know how to live.

Johann Wolfgang von Goethe, German writer and statesman, 1749-1832

May 10

The only place where success comes before work is in the dictionary.

Vidal Sassoon, British hairstylist and businessman, 1928-2012

May 11

The truth is, everyone is going to hurt you.
You just got to find the ones worth
suffering for.

*Bob Marley, Jamaican musician, singer and
songwriter, 1945-1981*

May 12

Not all those who wander are lost.

JRR Tolkien (John Ronald Reue), British author, 1892-1973

May 13

If you set your goals ridiculously high and it's a failure, you will fail above everyone else's success.

James Cameron, Canadian film director, 1954-

May 14

We have two ears and one mouth so that we can listen twice as much as we speak.

Epictetus, Greek Stoic philosopher,
50-138AD

May 15

Do you know, it's funny, but I never thought of
being blind as a disadvantage, and I never
thought of being black as a disadvantage.

*Stevie Wonder, (Stevland Hardaway
Morris né Judkins), US musician, singer and
songwriter, 1950-*

May 16

What is now proved was once only imagined.

William Blake, British poet and artist, 1757-1827

May 17

Life is not a matter of holding good cards,
but of playing a poor hand well.

*Robert Louis Stevenson, British (Scottish)
author and poet, 1850-1894*

May 18

Hell is truth seen too late.

Thomas Hobbes, British philosopher and author, 1588-1679

May 19

All men dream, but not equally. Those who dream by night in the dusty recesses of their minds, wake in the day to find that it was vanity: but the dreamers of the day are dangerous men, for they act on their dreams with open eyes, to make them possible.

T.E. Lawrence (Thomas Edward), 'Lawrence of Arabia', British (Welsh) author and soldier, 1888-1935

May 20

In order to succeed, we must first believe that we can.

Nikos Kazantzakis, Greek (Cretan) author, 1883-1957

May 21

If you light a lamp for someone else, it will also brighten your path.

Attributed to Buddha (Siddhattha Gotama), Nepalese philosopher and spiritual leader, c 6th-5th centuries BC.

May 22

Only the ideas we actually live are of any value.

Herman Hesse, German author, 1877-1962

May 23

If only we'd stop trying to be happy, we could have a pretty good time.

Edith Wharton, American author, 1862-1937

May 24

Wise men speak because they have something to say; fools because they have to say something.

Plato, Greek philosopher, c. 427-347BC

May 25

Don't compare yourself with other people.
Compare yourself to who you were
yesterday.

*Jordan B. Peterson, Canadian
psychologist and author, 1962-*

May 26

I do not think there is any other quality so essential to success of any kind as the quality of perseverance. It overcomes almost everything, even nature.

John D. Rockefeller, American industrialist and businessman, 1839-1937

May 27

Man prefers to believe what he prefers to be true.

Francis Bacon, British philosopher, author and pioneering scientist, 1561-1626

May 28

Life is hard. After all, it kills you.

Katharine Hepburn, American actress, 1907-2003

May 29

You must do the things you think you cannot do.

Eleanor Roosevelt, US First Lady, diplomat and political activist, 1884-1962

May 30

Knowing yourself is the beginning of all wisdom.

Aristotle, Greek philosopher, 384- 322BC

May 31

In order for the light to shine so brightly,
the darkness must be present.

*Francis Bacon, British philosopher, author and
pioneering scientist, 1561-1626*

June 1

Everyone has a plan till they get punched in the mouth.

Mike Tyson (Michael Gerard), American former heavyweight boxing champion, 1966-

June 2

Reject your sense of injury and the injury itself disappears.

Marcus Aurelius, Roman emperor and Stoic philosopher, 121-180AD

June 3

He who is not courageous enough to take risks will accomplish nothing in life.

Muhammed Ali, (Cassius Marcellus Clay Jr.), American former heavyweight boxing champion and activist, 1942-2016

June 4

I never lose. I either win or I learn.

*Nelson Mandela, anti-apartheid activist and
South African President, 1918-2013*

June 5

A sure way to lose happiness, I found, is to want it at the expense of everything else.

Bette Davis, American actress,1908-1989

June 6

Never, never, never give up.

Sir Winston Churchill, British Prime Minister and writer, 1874-1965

June 7

The definition of freedom is being fearless.

Nina Simone, (Eunice Kathleen Waymon),
American pianist, singer, songwriter and
activist, 1933-2003

June 8

Life's too short to deal with other people's insecurities.

Sir Anthony Hopkins,
British (Welsh) actor, 1937-

June 9

A loving heart is the truest wisdom.

Charles Dickens, British author,
1812-1870

June 10

Life itself is the most wonderful
fairy tale.

*Hans Christian Andersen, Danish author,
1805-1875*

June 11

A long habit of not thinking a thing wrong, gives it a superficial appearance of being right.

Thomas Paine, British author, philosopher and American revolutionary, 1737-1809

June 12

I don't think of all the misery, but of the beauty that still remains.

Anne Frank, German-Dutch diarist,
1929-1945

June 13

The world of reality has its limits; the world of imagination is boundless.

Jean-Jacques Rousseau, French writer and political philosopher, 1712-1778

June 14

Many of life's failures are people who do not realise how close they were to success when they gave up.

Thomas Edison, American developer of inventions and businessman, 1847-1931

June 15

The measure may be thought bold, but I am of the opinion the boldest are the safest.

Lord Horatio Nelson, British admiral and war hero, 1758-1805

June 16

The secret of happiness is freedom, and the secret of freedom is courage.

Thucydides, Greek historian, c. 460-400BC

June 17

Keep away from those who try to belittle your ambitions. Small people always do that, but the really great make you believe that you too can become great.

Mark Twain, (Samuel Clemens), American author and humorist, 1835-1910

June 18

It is the mark of an educated mind to be able to entertain a thought without accepting it.

Aristotle, Greek philosopher, 384-322BC

June 19

Some people talk to animals. Not many listen though. That's the problem.

A.A. Milne, British author of
Winnie-the-Pooh, 1882-1956

June 20

If you want to be happy, set a goal that commands your thoughts, liberates your energy, and inspires your hopes.

Andrew Carnegie, British (Scottish) American industrialist, 1835-1919

June 21

You don't have to see the whole staircase,
just take the first step.

*Martin Luther (Michael) King Jr, US civil
rights activist and minister, 1929-1968*

June 22

Cleverness is not wisdom.

Euripides, Greek playwright and poet,
480-406BC

June 23

Nothing will ever be attempted if all possible objections must be first overcome.

Samuel Johnson, British writer and lexicographer, 1709-1784

June 24

The smallest minority on earth is the individual. Those who deny individual rights cannot claim to be defenders of minorities.

Ayn Rand, Russian-American author, 1905-1982

June 25

Human history becomes more and more a
race between education and catastrophe.

*H. G. Wells (Herbert George), British author,
1866-1946*

June 26

Well done is better than well said.

*Benjamin Franklin, American Founding
Father, polymath, author, politician, inventor
and scientist, 1705-1790*

June 27

Dying is easy. Comedy is difficult.

Edmund Gwenn, (Edmund John Kellaway),
British actor, 1877-1959

June 28

A wise man will make more opportunities than he finds.

Francis Bacon, British philosopher, author and pioneering scientist, 1561-1626

June 29

You cannot shake hands with a clenched fist.

Indira Gandhi, Indian Prime Minister, 1917-1984

June 30

Men's greatest weakness is their façade of strength, and women's greatest strength is their façade of weakness.

Warren Farrell, American political scientist and author, 1943-

July 1

Make voyages. Attempt them. There's nothing else.

Tennessee Williams (Thomas Larnier),
American playwright, 1911-1983

July 2

Art depends on luck and talent.

Francis Ford Coppola, US film director,
producer and screenwriter, 1939-

July 3

Remaining childish is a tremendous state of innocence.

John Lydon ('Johnny Rotten'), British singer and songwriter, 1956 –

July 4

Happiness is not a goal, it is a by-product.

Eleanor Roosevelt, US First Lady, diplomat and political activist, 1884-1962

July 5

When we remember we are all mad, the mysteries of life disappear and life stands explained.

Mark Twain, (Samuel Clemens), American author and humorist, 1835-1910

July 6

It is amazing how complete is the delusion that beauty is goodness.

Leo Tolstoy, Russian writer, 1828-1910

July 7

The most courageous act is still to think for yourself. Aloud.

Coco Chanel (Gabrielle Bonheur), French fashion designer and businesswoman, 1883-1971

July 8

Without freedom there can be no morality.

Carl Jung, Swiss psychiatrist and
psychoanalyst, 1875-1961

July 9

Some people dream of success, while others wake up and work hard at it.

Sir Winston Churchill, British Prime Minister and writer, 1874-1965

July 10

Everything you can imagine is real.

*Pablo Picasso, Spanish painter,
sculptor and ceramicist, 1881-1973*

July 11

It's discouraging to think how many people are shocked by honesty and how few by deceit.

Noël Coward, British playwright, composer, director, actor and singer, 1899-1973

July 12

Look for the ridiculous in everything, and you will find it.

Jules Renard, French author, 1864-1910

July 13

Happiness is a butterfly which, when pursued, is always just beyond your grasp, but which, if you will sit down quietly, may alight upon you.

Nathaniel Hawthorne, American author, 1804-1864

July 14

It has yet to be proven that intelligence has any survival value.

Arthur C. Clarke, British science-fiction writer, 1917-2008

July 15

It's a funny thing about life; if you refuse to accept anything but the best, you very often get it.

W. Somerset Maugham, British playwright and author, 1874-1965

July 16

To be truly great, one has to stand with people, not above them.

Montesquieu, (Charles-Louis de Secondat), French political philosopher, 1689-1755

July 17

The greater the artist, the greater the doubt. Perfect confidence is granted to the less talented as a consolation prize.

Robert Hughes, Australian art critic, 1938-2012

July 18

Have no fear of perfection. You'll never reach it.

Salvador Dali, Spanish
surrealist artist, 1904-1989

July 19

Judge a man by his questions rather than his answers.

Voltaire, (François-Marie Arouet), French writer and philosopher, 1694-1778

July 20

Keep love in your heart. A life without it is like a sunless garden where the flowers are dead.

Oscar Wilde, Anglo-Irish poet and playwright, 1854-1900

July 21

The worst part of success is trying to find someone who is happy for you.

Bette Midler, American singer, actress and comedian, 1945-

July 22

We all have dreams. But in order to make dreams come into reality, it takes an awful lot of determination, dedication, self-discipline, and effort.

Jesse Owens (James Cleveland), American athlete, 1913-1980

July 23

Remember that the most beautiful things in the world are the most useless; peacocks and lilies for instance.

John Ruskin, British art critic and writer, 1819-1900

July 24

There is nothing on this earth more to be prized than true friendship.

Thomas Aquinas, Italian priest, philosopher and theologian, 1225-1274

July 25

The time to repair the roof is when the sun is shining.

John F. Kennedy, American President, 1917-1963

July 26

It's all right letting yourself go, as long as you can get yourself back.

*Mick Jagger, British singer
and songwriter, 1943-*

July 27

The whole of life is coming to terms with yourself and the natural world. Why are you here? How do you fit in? What's it all about?

Sir David Attenborough, British naturalist, author and broadcaster, 1926 -

July 28

The world is a book, and those who do not travel read only a page.

Saint Augustine (of Hippo), theologian, philosopher and bishop, 354-430AD

July 29

What would life be if we had no courage to attempt anything?

Vincent Van Gogh, Dutch painter,
1853-1890

July 30

Knowing is not enough; we must apply.
Willing is not enough; we must do.

*Johann Wolfgang von Goethe, German writer
and statesman, 1749-1832*

July 31

If you live each day as if it were your last, someday you'll be right.

Steve Jobs, American businessman, inventor and designer 1955-2011

August 1

Do not go where the path may lead. Go instead where there is no path and leave a trail.

Ralph Waldo Emerson, American writer and philosopher, 1803-1882

August 2

Don't underestimate the value of Doing Nothing, of just going along, listening to all the things you can't hear, and not bothering.

A.A. Milne, British author of
Winnie-the-Pooh, 1882-1956

August 3

Imagination is everything. It is the preview of life's coming attractions.

Albert Einstein, German-born theoretical physicist, 1879-1955

August 4

It is only with the heart that one can see rightly; what is essential is invisible to the eye.

Antoine de Saint-Exupéry, French writer and aviator, 1900-1944

August 5

The only constant in life is change.

Heraclitus (of Ephesus),
Greek philosopher, c. 535-475BC

August 6

It's no wonder that truth is stranger than fiction. Fiction has to make sense.

Mark Twain, (Samuel Clemens), American author and humorist, 1835-1910

August 7

Our greatest weakness is giving up. The most certain way to succeed is always to try just one more time.

Thomas Edison, American developer of inventions and businessman, 1847-1931

August 8

The greatest danger for most of us lies not in setting our aim too high and falling short; but in setting our aim too low, and achieving our mark.

*Michelangelo (di Lodovico Buonarroti Simoni),
Italian sculptor, painter and architect,
1475-1564*

August 9

Life goes by fast. Enjoy it. Calm down. It's all funny. Everyone gets so upset about the wrong things.

Joan Rivers, American comedian, 1933-2014

August 10

Life is thickly sown with thorns, and I know of no other remedy than to pass quickly through them. The longer we dwell on our misfortunes, the greater is their power to harm us.

Voltaire, (François-Marie Arouet), French writer and philosopher, 1694-1778

August 11

Life is a great big canvas; throw all the
paint you can at it.

Danny Kaye, (David Daniel Kaminsky),
American actor, singer and comedian,
1911-1987

August 12

Even if you are a minority of one, the truth is the truth.

Mahatma Gandhi (Mohandas Karamchand), Indian nationalist, lawyer and ethicist, 1869-1948

August 13

Failure is simply the opportunity to begin again, this time more intelligently.

Henry Ford, American industrialist and businessman, 1863-1947

August 14

Experience is not what happens to you; it is what you do with what happens to you.

Aldous Huxley, British writer and philosopher, 1894-1963

August 15

It is easy to be brave from a safe distance.

Aesop, Greek story-teller, ex-slave and
attributed author of fables, 620-564BC

August 16

I don't know anything about music.

Elvis Presley, American singer, musician and actor, 1935-1977

August 17

Take rest; a field that has rested gives a bountiful crop.

Ovid, (Publius Ovidius Naso),
Roman poet, 43BC-17AD

August 18

The trouble with the world is that the stupid are cocksure and the intelligent full of doubt.

Bertrand Russell, British philosopher and polymath, 1872-1970

August 19

Do not consider painful what is good for you.

Euripides, Greek playwright and poet, 480-406BC

August 20

If life had a second edition, how I would correct the proofs.

John Clare, British poet,1793-1864

August 21

The true object of all human life is play.

*G.K. Chesterton (Gilbert Keith), British writer
and philosopher,1874-1936*

August 22

Knowledge is of no value unless you put it into practice.

Anton Chekhov, Russian playwright and short story writer, 1860-1904

August 23

Most of the evil in this world is done by people with good intentions.

T.S. Eliot (Thomas Stearns), American-born British author and poet, 1888-1965

August 24

The hottest places in hell are reserved for those who, in times of great moral crisis, maintain their neutrality.

John F. Kennedy, (after Dante), American President, 1917-1963

August 25

Doing nothing is very hard to do. You never know when you're finished.

Leslie Nielsen, Canadian actor and comedian, 1926-2010

August 26

The unexamined life is not worth living.

Socrates, Greek philosopher,c. 469-399BC

August 27

I can calculate the motion of heavenly bodies but not the madness of people.

Sir Isaac Newton, British physicist,
mathematician and author, 1643-1727

August 28

Tolerance is only another name for indifference.

W. Somerset Maugham, British playwright and author, 1874-1965

August 29

Good artists copy; great artists steal.

Pablo Picasso, Spanish painter,
sculptor and ceramicist, 1881-1973

August 30

Tact is the ability to describe others as they see themselves.

Abraham Lincoln, American President, 1809-1865

August 31

Only do what your heart tells you.

Diana, Princess of Wales, 1961-1997

September 1

Courage is the most important virtue
because it makes all others possible.

*Winston Churchill, British Prime Minister
and writer, 1874-1965*

September 2

If you want to live a happy life, tie it to a goal, not to people or things.

Albert Einstein, German-born theoretical physicist, 1879-1955

September 3

The best revenge is massive success.

Frank Sinatra, American singer and actor, 1915-1998

September 4

If you can't tolerate critics, don't do anything new or interesting.

Jeff Bezos (Jorgensen), American businessman and internet entrepreneur, 1964-

September 5

Dullness is a disease.

Freddie Mercury, (Farrokh Bulsara), British musician, singer and songwriter, 1946-1991

September 6

Don't be late for whatever you want to be in time for.

A.A. Milne, British author of Winnie-the-Pooh, 1882-1956

September 7

The two most important days of your life are the day you were born and the day you find out why.

Anonymous (often misattributed to Mark Twain, American author and humorist, 1835-1910)

September 8

Try to learn something about everything and everything about something.

Thomas Henry Huxley, British biologist and anthropologist, 1825-1895

September 9

Those that know, do. Those that understand, teach.

Aristotle, Greek philosopher, 384-322BC

September 10

If you think you can win, you can win.
Faith is necessary to victory.

*William Hazlitt, British writer and
philosopher,1778-1830*

September 11

If we live in fear of hell, we have it.

Anonymous

September 12

It's not that I'm afraid to die. I just don't want to be there when it happens.

Woody Allen, (Allan Stewart Konigsberg), American film director, actor, comedian and writer, 1935-

September 13

No man ever steps in the same river twice, for it's not the same river and he's not the same man.

Heraclitus (of Ephesus),
Greek philosopher, c. 535-475BC

September 14

This I know – that I know nothing.

Plato, Greek philosopher, c. 427-347BC

September 15

It's better to explore life and make mistakes than to play it safe. Mistakes are part of the dues one pays for a full life.

Sophia Loren, (Sofia Villani Scicolone), Italian actress, 1934-

September 16

No people are uninteresting.

Yevgeny Yevtushenko, Russian poet,
1933-2017

September 17

Loneliness is and always has been the central and inevitable experience of every man.

Thomas Wolfe, American novelist, 1900-1938

September 18

It's funny how most people love the dead;
once you're dead, you're made for life.

*Jimi Hendrix (James Marshall; né Johnny
Allen), American musician, guitarist, singer
and songwriter, 1942-1970*

September 19

For every evil under the sun
There's a remedy, or there's none.
If there is one, go and find it.
If there is none, never mind it.

Mother Goose Nursey Rhymes,
18th century or earlier.

September 20

Age is something that doesn't matter,
unless you are a cheese.

Luis Buñuel, Spanish film director, 1900-1983

September 21

Your time is limited, so don't waste it
living someone else's life.

*Steve Jobs, American businessman, inventor
and designer 1955-2011*

September 22

We're born alone, we live alone, we die alone. Only through our love and friendship can we create the illusion for the moment that we're not alone.

Orson Welles, US film director, producer, screenwriter and actor, 1915-85

September 23

Do every act of your life as if it were your last.

Marcus Aurelius, Roman emperor and Stoic philosopher, 121-180AD

September 24

Life isn't about finding yourself. Life is about creating yourself.

George Bernard Shaw, Irish playwright, 1856-1950

September 25

Always be a first-rate version of yourself, instead of a second-rate version of somebody else.

Judy Garland, (Frances Ethel Gumm), American actress and singer, 1922-1969

September 26

Don't judge each day by the harvest you reap, but by the seeds you plant.

Robert Louis Stevenson, British (Scottish) author and poet, 1850-1894

September 27

The more powerful and original a mind, the more it will incline towards the religion of solitude.

Aldous Huxley, British writer and philosopher,1894-1963

September 28

The privilege of a lifetime is being who you are.

Joseph Campbell, American author on comparative mythology, 1904-87

September 29

All oppression creates a state of war.

Simone de Beauvoir, French writer, feminist, activist and philosopher, 1908-1986

September 30

There is much pleasure to be gained from useless knowledge.

Bertrand Russell, British philosopher and polymath, 1872-1970

October 1

We must adjust to changing times and still hold unchanging principles.

Jimmy Carter (James Earl Carter Jr.), American President, 1924-

October 2

Before you judge a man, walk a mile in his shoes. After that, who cares? He's a mile away and you've got his shoes!

Billy Connolly, British (Scottish) comedian, actor and musician, 1942-

October 3

Progress is man's ability to complicate simplicity.

Thor Heyerdahl, Norwegian explorer and ethnologist, 1914-2002

October 4

We can judge the heart of a man by his treatment of animals.

Immanuel Kant, German philosopher, 1724-1804

October 5

The only man who never makes mistakes is the man who never does anything.

Theodore 'Teddy' Roosevelt, American President, 1858-1919

October 6

I am not young enough to know everything.

James M. Barrie, British (Scottish) author, 1860-1937

October 7

One of the most beautiful qualities of true friendship is to understand and to be understood.

Seneca (Lucius Annaeus), Roman Stoic philosopher and statesman, 4BC-65AD

October 8

Find a place inside where there's joy, and the joy will burn out the pain.

Joseph Campbell, American author on comparative mythology, 1904-87

October 9

We act as though comfort and luxury were the chief requirements of life, when all we need to make us really happy is something to be enthusiastic about.

Charles Kingsley, British author, 1819-1875

October 10

Where words fail, music speaks.

Hans Christian Andersen, Danish author,
1805-1875

October 11

A friend is someone who gives you total freedom to be yourself.

Jim Morrison, American singer and songwriter, 1943-1971

October 12

Hope is a good breakfast, but it is a bad supper.

Francis Bacon, British philosopher, author and pioneering scientist, 1561-1626

October 13

Real knowledge is to know the extent of one's ignorance.

Confucius, (Kong Fuzi), Chinese philosopher, 551-479BC

October 14

Be patient toward all that is unsolved in your heart.

Rainer Maria Rilke (René), Czech-born German poet and novelist, 1875-1926

October 15

It is not necessary for eagles to be crows.

*Sitting Bull, (T̆hat̆háŋka Íyotake), Native
American (Hunkpapa Lakota) leader,
1831-1890*

October 16

The wisest men follow their own direction.

Euripides, Greek playwright and poet,
480-406BC

October 17

Those who do not want to imitate
anything, produce nothing.

*Salvador Dali, Spanish
surrealist artist, 1904-1989*

October 18

Political correctness is tyranny with manners.

Charlton Heston, American actor and Activist, 1923-2008

October 19

The value of life lies not in the length of days but in the use we make of them.

Michel de Montaigne, French philosopher and essayist, 1533-1592

October 20

Questions you cannot answer are usually far better for you than answers you cannot question.

Yuval Noah Harari, Israeli historian, philosopher and author, 1976-

October 21

Nobody knows anything.

William Goldman, American novelist and screenwriter,1931-2018

October 22

If Liberty means anything at all, it means the right to tell people what they do not want to hear.

George Orwell, (Eric Arthur Blair), British author and journalist, 1903-1950

October 23

All war is a symptom of man's failure as a thinking animal.

John Steinbeck, American author, 1902-1968

October 24

Be obscure clearly.

E.B. White (Elwyn Brooks), American author,
1899-1985

October 25

Use your health, even to the point of wearing it out. That is what it is for. Spend all you have before you die; do not outlive yourself.

George Bernard Shaw, Irish playwright, 1856-1950

October 26

Most of the noise always seems to come from the shallow end of the swimming pool.

Anonymous

October 27

In ancient times cats were worshipped as gods; they have not forgotten this.

Terry Pratchett, British satirical author,
1948-2015

October 28

I hope for nothing. I fear for nothing. I am free.

Nikos Kazantzakis, Greek (Cretan) author, 1883-1957

October 29

Pay no attention to what the critics say. No statue has ever been erected to a critic.

Jean Sibelius (Johan Julius Christian), Finnish composer, 1865-1957

October 30

Anyone can get old. All you have to do is live long enough.

Groucho Marx (Julius Henry), American comedian, actor and writer, 1890-1977

October 31

There is no sun without shadow, and it is essential to know the night.

Albert Camus, French author and philosopher, 1913-1960

November 1

It takes courage to grow up and become who you really are.

E.E. Cummings (Edward Estlin), American poet, 1894-1962

November 2

No-one can make you feel inferior without your consent.

Eleanor Roosevelt, US First Lady, diplomat and political activist, 1884-1962

November 3

Where knowledge ends, religion begins.

Benjamin Disraeli, British Prime Minister and novelist, 1804-1881

November 4

Funny thing is that the poorer people are, the more generous they seem to be.

Dolly Parton, American singer, songwriter and actress, 1946-

November 5

Death is one moment, and life is so many
of them.

*Tennessee Williams (Thomas Larnier),
American playwright, 1911-1983*

November 6

You only live once, but if you do it right,
once is enough.

Mae West (Mary Jane), American actress,
playwright and screenwriter, 1893-1980

November 7

If you never change your mind, why have one?

Edward de Bono, Maltese author and philosopher, originator of 'lateral thinking', 1933-2021

November 8

Comedy is simply a funny way of being serious.

Peter Ustinov, British actor and author, 1921-2004

November 9

When one burns one's bridges, what a very
nice fire it makes.

Dylan Thomas, British (Welsh) poet,
1914-1953

November 10

A person starts dying when they stop dreaming.

William Blake, British poet and artist, 1757-1827

November 11

Death does not concern us, because as long as we exist, death is not here. And when it does come, we no longer exist.

Epicurus (Epikouros), Greek philosopher, 341-270BC

November 12

Diplomacy is the art of letting someone else have your way.

David Frost, British journalist, writer and TV host, 1939-2013

November 13

It is only when they go wrong that machines remind you how powerful they are.

Clive James, Australian author and broadcaster, 1939-2019

November 14

Life would be tragic if it weren't funny.

Stephen Hawking, British physicist and author, 1942-2018

November 15

I am certain there is too much certainty in the world.

Michael Crichton, American author and film director, 1942-2008

November 16

Man sacrifices health to make money; then he sacrifices money to recuperate his health… He lives as if he is never going to die, and then dies having never really lived.

The Dalai Lama XIV (né Lhamo Döndrub),
Buddhist monk, 1935-

November 17

Happiness is good health and a bad memory.

Ingrid Bergman, Swedish actress,
1915-1982

November 18

Vision is the art of seeing what is invisible to others.

Jonathan Swift, Anglo-Irish satirist and author, 1667-1745

November 19

The only way to do great work is to love what you do.

Steve Jobs, American businessman, inventor and designer 1955-2011

November 20

It's kind of fun to do the impossible.

*Walt Disney, American animator and film
producer, 1901-1966*

November 21

He who seeks equality between unequals
seeks an absurdity.

*Baruch (Benedictus de) Spinoza, Dutch
philosopher, 1632-1677*

November 22

Efforts and courage are not enough without purpose and direction.

John F. Kennedy, American President, 1917-1963

November 23

Friendship is like a glass ornament, once it is broken it can rarely be put back together exactly the same way.

Charles Kingsley, British author, 1819-1875

November 24

To appreciate the beauty of a snowflake, it is necessary to stand out in the cold.

Aristotle, Greek philosopher,
384-322BC

November 25

Anything can become excusable when seen from the standpoint of the result.

Yukio Mishima, (Kimitake Hiraoka), Japanese author, 1925-1970

November 26

Comparison is the thief of joy.

Theodore 'Teddy' Roosevelt, American President, 1858-1919

November 27

You are never too old to set another goal or to dream a new dream.

C.S. Lewis (Clive Staples), British writer, 1898-1963

November 28

Trust your own instinct. Your mistakes might as well be your own, instead of someone else's.

Billy Wilder, Polish-American film director and screenwriter, 1906-2002

November 29

We live as we dream – alone.

Joseph Conrad, (Józef Teodor Konrad Korzeniowski), Polish-British author, 1857-1924

November 30

Live your own life, for you will die your own death.

Ancient Roman proverb

December 1

The meaning of life is that it ends.

*Franz Kafka, German-Czech author,
1883-1924*

December 2

I want to live my life so that my nights are not so full of regrets.

D.H. Lawrence (David Herbert), British author and poet, 1885-1930

December 3

Life shrinks or expands in proportion to one's courage.

Anaïs Nin, French-Cuban-American writer, 1903-1977

December 4

A gem cannot be polished without friction, nor a man perfected without trials.

Seneca (Lucius Annaeus), Roman Stoic philosopher and statesman, 4BC-65AD

December 5

Friends show their love in times of trouble, not in happiness.

Euripides, Greek playwright and poet, 480-406BC

December 6

What is important is seldom urgent, and what is urgent is seldom important.

Dwight D. Eisenhower, American President and army general, 1890-1969

December 7

Just because nobody complains doesn't
mean all parachutes are perfect.

*Benny Hill (Alfred Hawthorne), British
comedian, 1924-1992*

December 8

Reality leaves a lot to the imagination.

John (Winston Ono) Lennon, British
songwriter and musician, 1940-1980

December 9

Grief is the price we pay for love.

Colin Murray Parkes, British psychiatrist and author, 1928-

December 10

Give up defining yourself – to yourself or to others. You won't die. You will come to life.

Eckhart Tolle, (Ulrich Leonard Tölle), German author and spiritual teacher, 1948-

December 11

Turn your wounds into wisdom.

Oprah Winfrey, American talk-show host and TV producer, 1954-

December 12

Those who have knowledge, don't predict.
Those who predict, don't have knowledge.

Attributed to Lao Tzu, semi-legendary Chinese Taoist philosopher, exact dates unknown but 6th-4th century BC.

December 13

The groundwork of all happiness is health.

Leigh Hunt, British poet and essayist,
1784-1859

December 14

If you fell down yesterday, stand up today.

H. G. Wells (Herbert George), British author,
1866-1946

December 15

Nothing is particularly hard if you divide it into small jobs.

Henry Ford, American industrialist and businessman, 1863-1947

December 16

It is better to be alone than in bad company.

George Washington, American President, 1732-1799

December 17

Fortune favours the brave.

Terence, (Publius Terentius Afer),
Roman playwright, 195-159BC

December 18

The pain I feel now is the happiness I had before. That's the deal.

C.S. Lewis (Clive Staples), British writer, 1898-1963

December 19

Nothing is permanent in this wicked world
– not even our troubles.

*Charlie Chaplin, British comic actor, film
director, screenwriter, composer,
1889-1977*

December 20

The more I study religions, the more I am convinced that man never worshipped anything but himself.

Richard Francis Burton, British explorer and writer, 1821-1890

December 21

You never really know your friends from
your enemies until the ice breaks.

Traditional Eskimo proverb

December 22

In the depth of winter I finally learned that there was in me an invincible summer.

Albert Camus, French author and philosopher, 1913-1960

December 23

Do not spoil what you have by desiring what you have not. Remember that what you have now was among the things you only hoped for.

Epicurus (Epikouros), Greek philosopher, 341-270BC

December 24

Praise the God of all, drink the wine, and let the world be the world.

Traditional French proverb

December 25

There seems a magic in the very name of Christmas.

Charles Dickens, British author, 1812-1870

December 26

Every man is guilty of all the good he did not do.

Voltaire, (François-Marie Arouet), French writer and philosopher, 1694-1778

December 27

Kindness is in our power, even when
fondness is not.

*Samuel Johnson, British writer and
lexicographer, 1709-1784*

December 28

All we have to decide is what to do with
the time that is given us.

*JRR Tolkien (John Ronald Reue), British
author, 1892-1973*

December 29

It's not what happens to you, but how you react to it that matters.

Epictetus, Greek Stoic philosopher, 50-138AD

December 30

So may the New Year be a happy one to you, happy to many more whose happiness depends on you.

Charles Dickens, British author, 1812-1870

December 31

And now we welcome the new year, full of things that have never been.

Rainer Maria Rilke (René), Czech-born German poet and novelist, 1875-1926

ABOUT THE AUTHOR

Jem Vanston was born and brought up in Dartford, Kent. He now lives in Swansea.

As well as being an award-winning author and poet, he is a published songwriter, a sometime journalist and English teacher, an occasional film producer, and also runs his own training, writing and editing companies online.

Author website: www.vanston.co.uk

Fiction by the same author:

Crump (2010)
A Cat Called Dog (2013)
A Cat Called Dog (illustrated shorter version, 2015)
Rasmus – a Television Tale (2016)
A Cat Called Dog 2 – the one with the kittens (illustrated, 2017)
Santa Goes on Strike (illustrated, 2018)
Somewhere in Europe (2020)

Printed in Great Britain
by Amazon